YOGA FOR EVERYONE
STANDING YOGA

BY LAURA VILLANO, RYT
ILLUSTRATED BY CHRISTOS SKALTSAS

BLUE OWL
BOOKS

TIPS FOR CAREGIVERS

The practice of yoga helps us learn about our breath and body, how the two are connected, and how they can help us acknowledge our feelings without letting them overwhelm us. This awareness can help us navigate different situations at school or at home. Yoga gives us tools to be the best versions of ourselves in every situation. Plus, moving our bodies feels good!

SOCIAL AND EMOTIONAL GOALS

After reading this book, kids will be able to use their yoga practice to:

1. Become more aware of their emotions and the physical sensations they produce in the body (self-awareness).

2. Use the techniques included in the text to help manage their emotions and de-stress (self-management).

TIPS FOR PRACTICE

Encourage self-awareness and self-management with these prompts:

Before reading: Ask students to check in with themselves. How do they feel, in both mind and body?
Emotional example: What kinds of thoughts are you having?
Physical example: How does your body feel today?

During reading: Encourage students to check in as they move through the book.
Emotional example: How does it feel when you close your eyes and focus on your breathing?
Physical example: How do certain poses feel in your body?

After reading: Take time to reflect after practicing the poses.
Emotional example: How do you feel after practicing yoga?
Physical example: Are there certain poses you like or don't like?

TABLE OF CONTENTS

BEFORE YOU BEGIN YOUR PRACTICE, YOU WILL NEED:

- Yoga mat (A towel or blanket works, too!)
- Comfy clothes so you can move around easily
- Wall or chair close by
- Water to stay hydrated
- A good attitude and an open mind!

By practicing the poses in this book, you understand any physical activity has some risk of injury.
If you experience pain or discomfort, please listen to your body, discontinue activity, and ask for help.

CHAPTER 1

WHAT IS YOGA?

Namaste (nah-mah-stay)! This is how we greet each other when we practice **yoga**. We place our palms together in front of our chest. We bow our heads. In this book, you will learn **poses** you can do while standing.

❯ Start by putting your hand on your stomach.

❯ **Inhale** through your nose. Feel the air fill up your belly.

❯ **Exhale**. Feel your belly relax as the air leaves your nose.

❯ Repeat this 10 times.

As you move through the book, **focus** on your breathing.

CHAPTER 2

LET'S PRACTICE!

MOUNTAIN POSE

❯ Start at the top of your mat.

❯ Keep your arms by your sides. Point your fingertips toward the floor.

❯ Draw your shoulders down your back.

FORWARD FOLD

❯ Breathe in and reach your arms overhead.

❯ Exhale and fold forward.

❯ Reach toward the floor. Let your head hang heavy.

❯ Do you feel the stretch in the back of your legs?

❯ Hold this pose for 5 breaths.

DOWNWARD-FACING DOG PART 1

Let's **flow** into the next pose.

▶ Inhale. As you exhale, plant your hands on the mat.

▶ Step your feet back one at a time until you are in a high plank position.

DOWNWARD-FACING DOG PART 2

❱ Press down firmly with your hands.

❱ Lift your hips up and back toward your heels.

❱ Look back at your feet.

❱ Your body should look like an upside-down V!

TIP: Focus on relaxing your shoulders.

CHAIR POSE

❱ Inhale and look up toward the edge of your mat.

❱ Exhale and walk your feet to your hands. Now you are back in Forward Fold!

❱ Bend your knees.

❱ On your next inhale, reach your arms up over your head.

❱ Keep your knees bent!

❱ Hold this pose for 5 breaths. Do you feel your leg muscles working?

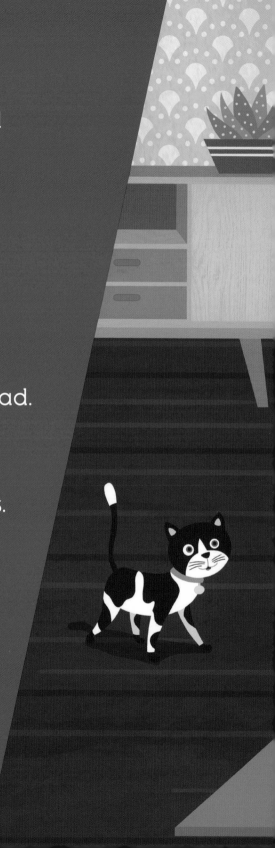

TIP: Don't lean forward on your toes! Keep your weight in your heels.

HIGH LUNGE

❱ Go back to Mountain Pose.

❱ Bring your hands to your hips.

❱ Stand strong.

❱ Inhale and step your left foot behind you.

❱ Bend your right knee.

❱ Keep your left leg strong and straight.

❱ Reach your arms above your head.

TIP: Your right knee should line up with your ankle.

WARRIOR 2

❯ Inhale. As you exhale, turn to face the long side of your mat.

❯ Your left foot should now face the long side of the mat. Your toes on your right foot should point to the short end.

❯ Raise your arms out to the sides. Keep them level with your shoulders. Face your palms down.

❯ Turn your head to the right. Look past your fingertips.

❯ Hold this pose for 3 to 5 breaths. How does your body feel?

TIP: Press down with your back foot. This will help you balance.

TRIANGLE POSE

❱ Keep your feet in the same position.

❱ Straighten your right leg.

❱ Inhale. Exhale and bring your right hand down near your right calf or ankle.

❱ Reach your left fingertips to the sky.

❱ Turn your head so you are looking up toward your left-hand fingers.

❱ Keep your chest faced outward.

❱ Now try these poses on the other side!

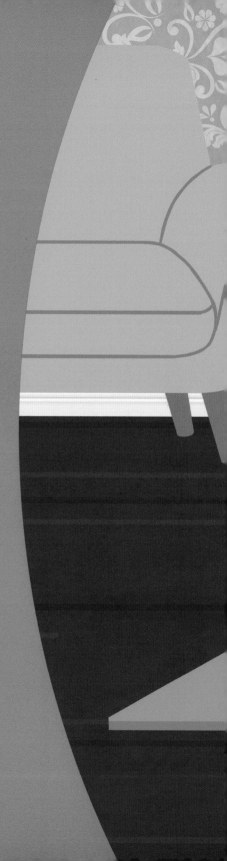

TIP: Don't forget to breathe! Your body is working hard! Take your time. Focus on moving slowly with your breath into each pose.

CHAPTER 3

REFLECT

Let's finish our standing yoga practice.

❯ Stand tall in Mountain Pose.

❯ Close your eyes.

❯ Inhale and exhale 5 times.

❯ Take time to **reflect**. How do you feel?

Namaste!

Now you know standing poses! What pose is your favorite? Keep practicing. You can teach your friends!

GOALS AND TOOLS

GROW WITH GOALS

Practice bringing yoga into your everyday life.
Here are some ideas to get you started!

1. Pick a standing yoga pose that was challenging. Practice this pose 3 times a week. Notice how this pose feels the more you do it. What stays the same? What changes?

2. Practice Downward-Facing Dog 3 times a week. Stretch your heels back a bit farther each time. Can you touch your heels to the floor?

TRY THIS!

Explore different versions of Chair Pose with a friend!

Option 1: Stand back-to-back with your yoga partner. Link your elbows together. Slowly bend your knees and lower into your Chair Poses.

Option 2: Stand facing your yoga partner. Stand about an arms-length away from each other. Reach out and hold hands. Make sure you have a good grip! Slowly bend your knees and lower into your Chair Poses.

Reflect: How did these partner poses compare to Chair Pose on your own? What was challenging? Did you like it? Did the poses work different muscles?

GLOSSARY

exhale
To breathe out.

flexible
Able to bend.

flow
To transition slowly from one yoga pose to another.

focus
To concentrate on something.

inhale
To breathe in.

namaste
A common greeting in yoga. It means, "The spirit in me honors and acknowledges the spirit in you."

poses
Positions or postures.

reflect
To think carefully or seriously about something.

yoga
A system of exercises and meditation that helps people control their minds and bodies and become physically fit.

TO LEARN MORE

Finding more information is as easy as 1, 2, 3.

1. Go to www.factsurfer.com

2. Enter "**standingyoga**" into the search box.

3. Choose your cover to see a list of websites.

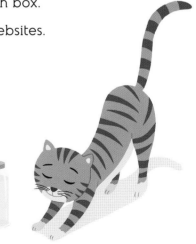

INDEX

Blue Owl Books are published by Jump!, 5357 Penn Avenue South, Minneapolis, MN 55419, www.jumplibrary.com

Copyright © 2020 Jump! International copyright reserved in all countries. No part of this book may be reproduced in any form without written permission from the publisher.

Library of Congress Cataloging-in-Publication Data

Names: Villano, Laura, author.
Title: Standing yoga / Laura Villano.
Description: Blue Owl Books. | Minneapolis, MN: Jump!, Inc., [2020]
Series: Yoga for everyone
Includes index.
Audience: Ages 7–10.
Identifiers: LCCN 2019021557 (print)
LCCN 2019981608 (ebook)
ISBN 9781645271901 (hardcover)
ISBN 9781645271918 (paperback)
ISBN 9781645271925 (ebook)
Subjects: LCSH: Hatha yoga for children—Juvenile literature.
Classification: LCC RJ133.7 .V55 2020 (print)
LCC RJ133.7 (ebook)
DDC 613.7/046083—dc23
LC record available at https://lccn.loc.gov/2019021557
LC ebook record available at https://lccn.loc.gov/2019981608

Editor: Jenna Trnka
Designer: Anna Peterson
Illustrator: Christos Skaltsas

Printed in the United States of America at Corporate Graphics in North Mankato, Minnesota.